CONTENTS

Introduction

WE ARE LIVING in the middle of a pandemic and we are self isolating ourselves in our homes in lockdown. Fuel prices have dropped, social distancing rules are in place, tape on the floor at supermarkets, a limited number of people in shops, panic buying of toilet rolls, pasta and flour.

Concerts, festivals, weddings and celebrations all cancelled. Schools are closed, no meeting up with friends, we are told to self isolate yourself at home, and no socialising with anyone outside your home.

We are washing our hands many times through the day leaving them sore and dry and trying not to touch our faces, which is a lot more difficult than I ever would have realised.

There are rainbows and teddy bears in windows for the children to see on their allocated daily walk with their family and we all clap on a Thursday evening to let the NHS we appreciate all that they are doing.

Non-essential shops and businesses are closed and the world is currently changing on a daily basis.

It's a strange and worrying time and bringing in a new puppy in your home should be a source of relief and joy, but for many puppy new owners all over the county, it may be causing stress and worry. As when you had planned on getting your new puppy before any of this happened, you expected to be able to attend puppy classes and take your puppy to the park as and when you wished.

1

The world we are living in has restrictions that are in place for our own safety, including only one form of exercise per day and social distancing — how will you ensure your puppy grows up to be that dream dog you envisioned?

It's such a critical period for your puppy and the worry about getting it wrong can be stress you really don't need at the moment.

Puppy training classes are shut, no puppy parties at the vets and you have so many questions about how to raise your puppy:

- How do we stop him biting my hands?
- How do I stop her from going to the toilet in my house?
- How do I get her to sleep through the night without crying?
- How do I train her with no classes open?
- And with social distancing in place, you are worried about how you will socialise your puppy when you are not allowed to go near anyone or their dogs?
- How will you get them used to the world with only one form of exercise allowed each day?

Will my puppy end up being too attached to me with me working from home all the time and cause problems when I go back to work?

When you got your new puppy, socialisation is a word that you're breeder, your vet and you will be reading about in many books and magazine that you need to cram in socialisation when they are young or you won't end up with a good older dog. But in fact, many people have a little understanding of what socialisation actually means for your puppy.

If you look up the word socialisation there are two meaning to socialisation — one is 'activity of mixing socially with others' which is what people tend to focus on, when in fact what we need to focus on for our puppies is the other meaning, which is 'the process of learning to behave in a way that is acceptable to society'.

We need to teach our puppies to behave in a socially acceptable manner when in public and in the world we are living in.

THE PERFECT PUPPY POCKET PLAN

3 Easy Steps to Safely Raise Your Puppy in a Social Distancing World

Carrie Stuthridge

ISBN: 9798645657703

Puppies go through many development stages as they grow, just as we do. When they are aged 3-16 weeks they go through a sensitive period, where they are prime and open to the new experiences. It is important during this time period to work on socialising and habituating our puppies to ensure we build up a bank of positive experiences, but bear in mind it doesn't stop there, it does go on for the first two years of his life.

It actually starts through before you get your puppy home, whilst your puppy is still with your breeder, so making sure your puppy comes from a good breeder is very important to give them the best start in life.

Right now through, you have your puppy home in this sensitive period, whilst we are in lockdown — how can you make sure you create that bombproof puppy, that puppy that can take life in his stride and look at new experiences as a positive one?

This short book will take you on a journey with your new puppy through socialisation, habituation and crate training to help you raise your puppy during the lockdown and create that bombproof dog you were dreaming of. We want to make sure that they grow into an adult dog who is a pleasure to own and the envy of your friends.

My Story and how my puppy training secrets will help you

HOW MY LIFE got flipped, turned upside down and how I turned my passion and dream to become a reality

You get told when you are younger to study hard so you can get an awesome job. Advice comes from everywhere that you need to find a job you love, something you look forward to, a job that pays well.

At 16 I really didn't know what I wanted to do, I wasn't keen on staying on to do my A levels at school and decided to go for a career in fashion. I went to Coventry Technical College and then onto Lincoln University where I came out with a Fashion Studies BA (Hons) degree.

What they don't share with you that it's hard to get a job even with a degree behind you. I ended up working through various jobs whilst living in Lincoln from working in a music shop, for an insurance company, a sandwich shop, directory enquiries and a parcel delivery company to just name a few. Life was good, I enjoyed living there, but it got to a point where I knew I need to try and use my degree and get a career I would love rather than jumping from one job to the next and never being truly happy in a job.

The decision was made to move back to Coventry and I said that I would give it 2 years and if it didn't work out I could always move back to Lincoln.

Not long after moving back to Coventry, I got my first own dog Tye. It seemed the right time, we had a family dog, Crystal, when I was younger and I had always wanted to share my life again with a dog and whilst working in a pub when I was first back I had the time for a dog.

Crystal was a West Highland Terrier and we got her around my 8th birthday. I had begged and begged to get a dog, so when she came home I was over the moon. I remember going with my mum to classes at Massey Ferguson car park on a Sunday morning to teach her obedience. I don't remember going to many, but I imagine it was hard work trying to train a dog and trying to keep an eye on me too.

She was very much a family pet, didn't really know many behaviours apart from sit and down and she had to be walked on lead, as we never really sorted her recall out. Every chance she got if the front door was open, she would be out of it like a rocket and we would spend the next half an hour trying to catch her and bring her home.

She was a much loved family pet that was taken from us too early. A well meaning guest gave her a cooked lamb bone to eat, which made her very poorly. She had a few operations to remove the bone and to fix the damage it had caused, but she never recovered from them and died too young. I will always remember my nan dancing around the kitchen with her, as my nan loved her as much as I did.

My nan would have loved Tye too, as she was a dog lover like myself and I wish she knew the career I have ended up in. I adopted Tye from The Dogs Trust, he was classed as a Collie x but I think he may have had some German Shepard in him and some Flatcoat Retriever too from the size of him and how he looked.

Tye is one of the reasons I have ended up where I am now and why I became a dog trainer. He was a dog that taught me a lot from what not to do with a puppy to how to deal with a dog who barks and lunges at each dog he sees when he was older.

Tye had many 'normal' puppy problems, but at the time these were problems I just didn't know how to deal with which was stressful and frustrating at times. He was a stray from Ireland and was about 4 months old and would steal items from the side, thought it was a great game to run at me and bite and rip my coat and would jump up as he pleased. I knew I needed to fix these problems as when he would be fully grown he was going to end up a large dog.

We became partners in crime, he came everywhere he could with me, we went camping and on adventures together.

I had Tye for 2 years, before my time in Coventry was looking at coming to an end as I hadn't managed to get a career in the fashion industry. In that time I hard done bar work, waitressing and worked at outdoor shows selling clothing but still not loving any of the careers when I signed up at an agency and I got a job on a temporary contact with TU at Sainsbury's head office. This was it.

Fast forward 6 years through and my passion for it had died and I hated leaving super early in the morning and getting home late at night. I was not getting to spend much time with my dog as I wanted to and things needed to change. There are so many people that end up working for the weekend, wishing their lives away.

And this is what had happened to be me, waiting and wishing for the weekend to arrive to only wake up on Sunday and feel dread the weekend was nearly over. Not only was I missing out spending time with my dog, but I had fallen out of love with a job that I did love at one point, but no longer.

Mistakes started happening to a point where I had a meeting with my manager and she gave me two choices, go back to basics or go elsewhere.

When I came back in with my letter of resignation, her face dropped as this wasn't the outcome she was expecting. 'What are you going to do?' I am off to be a dog walker.

By that time, I was training to become a buyer. But, I had fallen out of love with the fashion industry and the corporate world just wasn't for me. Being stuck inside day after day in an office when all I wanted to spend more time with my dog Tye, be outside and work with dogs. I went away and researched what I could do and started applying to jobs to chase that dream.

A fresh beginning

I soon realised it wasn't easy to get a job working with dogs with no experience, I was getting the interviews, but it would stop there. When an of hand remark came one sunny afternoon, whilst drinking Pimms at a barbecue, when a family friend said 'Why don't you become a dog walker to gain the experience with dogs'. So that is just what I went out and did.

'You're so brave' and 'I wish I could make such a big change' were just a couple of the comments I received from friends at Sainsburys just before I left. I just knew this was not the life I wanted to lead, I no longer wanted to work in the fashion industry with my life mapped out, moving between companies. If I didn't make the change now, maybe I never would.

I don't mess around once a decision has been made and within a month I had a new job and was subcontracting dog walks from a dog walking & pet sitting company, covering a wide area of Coventry.

I loved being a dog walker, I got to spend all day taking care of other people dogs and at weekends I was also trusted to care for peoples cats whilst they took their weekends away and holidays.

Since I was a child I had always loved animals, especially dogs and why I didn't for-see a job with dogs until I was older, I will never know. It isn't a job for sure that the job advisors at school would push you towards. At last through, I had found the job I loved.

The first dog I walked was a mountain dog, talk about going in the deep end! I had met him at the meet and greet and everything had gone great, but when I walked in the house on why own to collect him for his first walk he just barked and barked at me. To have dog that size barking at you can be intimidating, but I knew what I needed to do was earn his trust with a gentle persuasion and a few treats, just as his owners had advised me to. Within 10 minutes we were off an I was on my first walk.

Over the first year I had the pleasure of walking collies to Rottweiler, long haired terriers to Dobermans. I was learning more about different breeds and it fascinated me and at the same time as much as I loved taking them out, I was wanting something more and started to think about what else can I do. As being a dog walker was supposed to be a stepping stone to my new career with dogs.

At the same time I was having trouble with my own dog, Tye. I used to take Tye on some of my walks, he got to meet the mountain dog, who made him look small and over time when I had a bigger lunchtime walk near my home, he would come and join me on that walk each day too.

He was great with the dogs on the walks and as he got in the van would say hi to everyone through the cages and he also loved his friends on out local walks. But something changed, he had started to bark and lunge and some dogs when we were out and coming in 48 kg he was hard to hold onto.

I knew I needed more help with him again and I had never really fixed his chase instinct, so wanted to fix that as well. After calling around many local trainers who answered and said 'yes I can help you' but some of the techniques they mentioned didn't sit right with me.

After mulling it over I started to think, why don't I just retrain myself to become a dog trainer and then I can help him, as he obviously is not happy and I want to be able to help him. I also had realised I had more than just an interest in fixing the problem I wanted to learn more about what was happening and why and how to help him and why it had changed. I managed his behaviour for a long time by keeping out the way of people we didn't know, but over time it did become more and more stressful.

I was already a frequent visitor of Crufts, so the next show came round and I visited all off the different organisations to decide who to train with, when I came across Angela White from IABTC.

The next year I studied dog training and behaviour intensely, visiting each month to Haxey to train with Angela and her team.

I found out Tye had become reactive to other dogs due to pain, he was just trying to protect himself, so with guidance I did a management and training programme with him to give him the best life I could.

Maisie also came into my life near the start of the course, Tye was getting older and not able to do everything I wanted to and I also wanted a puppy that I could watch grow and learn from. Maisie is a collie x spaniel as I wanted a dog I could use for demos and try different sports with too and has also taught me a lot and helped me on my training journey.

When I was near the end of my training with IABTC, the owner of the dog walking company did ask me to go into business with her as I had built up oboe the 2 years a good team covering most non Coventry. But it would have come with a change of job role for me and I decided it wasn't what I wanted to do, as it would take me further away from the dogs and I would just be training people and would be a waste of my new dog training skills.

My knee had started to play up at the end of 2015 due to all the walking I was doing, some days up to 30,000 steps, I was told I would need surgery to fix it. I decided this was a chance to make another big change, with the knee operation it would put me out of work for a few months whilst I recovered, I took this chance to leave and set up on my own, in March 2016 Carrie's Canines and Friends was born in March 2016.

Over the years I have attended various courses and seminars with some of the worlds leading dog trainers and behaviourists, which has helped me become the trainer I am today.

Over the past 4 years my business has changed and grown with me and down to hard work and determination and I am now Coventry's Number 1 Puppy Training Specialist using my Puppy Problem Prevention Programme to help first time puppy owners.

What is the Puppy Problem Prevention Programme?

Working with hundreds of owners and their new puppies, I have studied their behaviour and created a unique Puppy Problem Prevention Programme.

Working with owners and their new puppies, I have studied their behaviour and created a plan to ensure they end up with the dog they envisioned. Getting a new puppy is all cute and exciting, until they start peeing every where, chewing your furniture and keeping you up all night.

My proven training system stops that from happening.

It is much easier getting your puppy started off right from the start than trying to fix issues further down the line when the behaviours are more ingrained.

In this short book I'm going to share 3 key elements of my 10 step program that will help get you and your puppy through lockdown, so you come through it the other end of the pandemic with a confident and worry free dog.

1. Socialisation - How to socialise your dog with social distancing in place
2. Habituation - How to get your puppy used to the world and keeping their confidence high
3. Crate training - How to ensure he doesn't end up with separation issues

Socialisation - How to socialise your dog at a distance and get it right

QUALITY EXPERIENCES FOR your puppy, not quantity. You are mapping out the dog they will become.

I want you to think about what you envisioned when you decided to bring a dog into your family. Think about how you want your dog to be in different situations, what is their day to day life going to be like? Will they go to work with you or be at home? Do you enjoy going out for coffee and want them to join you? Do you like going camping and they will be going with you?

This is going to give you a start of what you need to work on and get your puppy used to so they are able to cope with life together with you.

Something I talk about, often, is how socialisation does not mean we need to get out there and introduce our puppies to every single dog going. We do not need to greet every aged person and one with a beard, one with a walking stick, children of all ages — as this is just not possible, even before lockdown happened never mind now.

What you need to work on first through is your bond with your new puppy, build a relationship with her. You need to be her right hand man, someone that she can turn to if she needs some reassurance or is worried by a situation.

Building Trust

Building that trust up with your puppy means if something worries them, they will run back to you or stick close to you. You want them to choose to feel safe and secure with you and that they can come back to you, you have their back when they need it.

You have spent time building your relationship with your puppy and what you need to do is to teach our puppies to behave in a socially acceptable manner when in public. What we are looking for and what you need for your puppies is for them to have positive outlook on life, we want them to go into a new experience and be excited, not worried.

We want them to go into a new experience and be excited, not worried.

The advised social distancing guidelines are actually a perfect way to socialise your puppy, without them becoming over faced or having them learn inappropriate social skills. Your goal for your puppy is to create a dog who is indifferent to 'things'. You want them to internally shrug their shoulders and be totally nonchalant about people, dogs, things. Social distancing is ideal for that. You don't need to have a battle or justify what you want people to just ignore you puppy, you just adhere to social distancing and this is going to create great focus from your puppy.

But what does this mean and what does it look like?

Imagine you are taking your puppy for the first time to the beach, this is a new experience for her she's not been there before. The smell of salt in the air, grains of sand under her paws, lots of people milling around eating ice cream, carrying buckets and spades, inflatables of all shapes and sizes, people in hats old and young. You want her to have a out look of

New experience = good stuff happens

The she takes it all in her stride and you spend the best afternoon with her at the beach.

If you don't spend the time building up that positive repose when they are young that trip to the beach would be very different.

You would have a puppy with a tail tucked under, cowering at your side not being able to deal with all the novelty around her. The ground feeling weird under her paws, people everywhere it all smells strange and not like home. A puppy that is desperate to get back in the car, a play of security.

How do we grow that confident puppy?

Let's start to look at interaction, how she interacts with the world around her and we need to build positive exposure to the world, but this all needs to be done at your puppy's own pace. No rushing your puppy or forcing them to get used to the environment around them, what this can do is overwhelm your puppy and cause stress and worry for them.

What we are doing with building the positive exposure to the world is building a bank of good experiences. There will be time when something less positive happens with your puppy, but by doing this we can ensure your puppy is going to be more resilient from that bad experience and recover quicker.

Giving your puppy the correct exposure is key to growing your bomb proof dog, so in my opinion the social distancing which is in place is going to do you and your puppy a huge favour right now.

Over exposure can create problems, as I first learnt with my first dog Tye.

Tye was my first own dog and for sure one that has a very special place in my heart. We had a family dog when I was younger called Crystal, even though she came home near my birthday and I had begged and pleaded for a dog for years it was my parents that did the care or her.

When I was 24, I moved back to Coventry after living in Lincoln for 6 years. Owning my own dog was something I had been dreaming of. I had visions of being an inseparable pair, going on walks together, entering agility competitions and being the best trained dog ever.

I was working in a pub at the time, so I had the time to bring a dog into the family and after persuading my parents that I would do everything from the feeding, care, training and walking it was agreed I could get a dog.

I was over the moon, at last a dog of my own.

This was a fair few years before I came a dog trainer, so really when choosing a dog to join the family I was looking for a dog that was easy to train and one that would join me on country adventures.

I didn't have a list of requirements, I didn't even have a particular breed in mind. I was just so happy to be eventually getting a dog of may own.

Tye was my dog that taught me a lot and he is also the reason I became a dog trainer.

The search was on, I wanted to re-home a puppy ideally and also wanted to rescue one from a charity, to give a dog a chance that had been given up by someone else.

There were a few dogs we looked at that day that I chose Tye at The Dogs Trust, but in my eye Tye shone above the rest with his crinkly ears, scrawny body and happy go lucky attitude as we walked him around to get to know him.

He for sure was the one I wanted to take home. He was reserved that day and came home with us less than a week later.

Research, research, research

I had read up on all books I could get my hands on, went to the library and took out all the book they had on dog training. I wanted to make sure after his bad start in life wandering the streets of Ireland, he would live the best life with me.

He was just 4 months old, you wouldn't have known by looking at him through as he was huge already. People kept saying he would need to grow into his paws, I did wonder at the time why I kept being told that - I now understand what they were saying!

Now he was home, I had read all my books from cover to cover and they were telling me I needed socialise him, to get him used to every dog and every person I could find, so I used his walks to seek them out.

He was the best dog, my socialisation had worked! He loved everyone and loved playing chase and games with any dog, but this soon became an issue.

When we would arrive at the park and he would see it as a time to go off and say 'hi' to each dog and everyone person around the park.

This very quickly escalated and soon become hard work. You would hear me shouting on a daily basis 'its ok he is friendly, just wants to say hi'. As he charged away from me to greet his new friend.

Walks became a nightmare

I soon learnt not every dog or person wants to say hi and it would often get me in trouble or I would be trying to grab onto him as soon as I saw someone coming to prevent him from running over.

This is one thing I have made sure with all of my dogs since, that I do not allow them to say hi to everyone when on a walk to prevent having recall issues every again from other dogs or people.

I need to be the best thing ever when I am out on a walk with them, not the rest of the environment.

So this is exactly what you need to be doing with your new puppy and why social distancing is actually great for you and your new puppy.

It will help teach them that yes there are other dogs and people here, but we don't need to be going over to bother them — they need to become what I call a non event, just something that happens on our walks and not to be overly interested about them.

Over Exposure

There are other issues that can arise from over exposure, one of them is too much dog to dog interaction, is it can be too much for a young puppy who is learning about the world.

This happened to Maisie when she was a puppy, we were out on a walk taking in the world when a larger dog spotted us across the field and starting making her way over to us.

She walked over at quite a slow pace, I was keeping my eye on Maisie but also fully aware this dog was homing in on us. Everything seemed fine and Maisie seemed comfortable, but then the game changed and the larger dog broke out into a sprint and came charging over. Before I had a chance to scoop her up out of the way her instincts had kicked in and Maisie had started to run and she was being chased with the big dog in hot pursuit. She was being chased in circles, her tail tucked under trying to get away from the larger dog, with me stood there watching, helpless. Maisie then made her way towards me so I took the chance and to quickly scooped her up into safety.

It was just too much for her, she hadn't felt comfortable in the situation. To this day when she sees that particular dog, she gets worried.

It can just be too much for puppies, so it must be all done at their pace. How do we do this?

What we want is for your puppy to decide when they are comfortable with a situation and you can help by giving them support and reassurance as and when they need it. You will learn to read your puppy and notice when she is comfortable in a situation as she will go closer and want to investigate or when she doesn't want to go any closer, she will back away and see you out for security and safety.

We need to work on building those positive associations with the world around her, whether that is people, children, other dogs — we want her to be comfortable with the world around her.

We need to let her experience these things from a safe distance and go at her pace.

Children

Lets look at children, if she wants to get closer to the children let her do at her pace, the handy situation we are currently in with social distancing is it is going to prevent kids surrounding her and this in turn will prevent her being overwhelmed by them. If a puppy get surrounded by children and they overwhelm her, it can potentially create a dog who is nervous of kids.

Remember you cannot reinforce fear, this is something we were always told that we must not comfort your dog as it would only reinforce it. You can comfort your puppy, if they need it. Just don't over dramatise the situation!

Tye became frightened by fireworks as he got older, something that would make me feel sick as he looked so frightened and scared. He would shake in fear, panting and pacing the room. I was told I must not comfort him as all this would do was reinforce to him that there was something to be frightened by.

I remember sitting there watching him searching for comfort thinking 'this just doesn't sit right' in the pit of my stomach I knew that I couldn't just sit there and ignore him, it didn't feel right. I tried my best to ignore and carry on like nothing was happening to eventually what I thought was giving in and comforting him.

I wish I had known what I know now and I would have just given him that comfort and support he was looking for, but hindsight is a fine thing.

Safe & Secure

What I want you to do with your puppy is to make sure your puppy feels safe and secure and can trust you. If they are looking for comfort and support, give it to them. Just be careful you don't over do it and end up over comforting them, making it a massive deal.

I know this may sound confusing, but just think of more exposure rather than interaction. The interaction can happen when your puppy is ready, in their time at their own pace.

This is why social distancing right now is your friend, you can get them used to seeing other dogs and people and they won't have the pressure of them coming over to your puppy as they can only say hi at a distance.

You need to think of your puppy as an individual with individual needs and take it all at their pace.

Whilst this is all in place too it is a fab time to practiser your polite greetings, practise your sit and greet with people and rewarding all calm and engagement with you around other people. This person can speak to the puppy as an extra challenge for you.

You need to think about what you need your dog to cope with in life, as they will be with you and your family for the next 10/15 for maybe more years.

Habituation - How to ensure you have a confident dog once we are back to normal

WE NEED TO work on habituation as well as socialisation, but what its habituation? It differs from socialisation as it is about the environment, inside and outside of your home — the sights, sounds, smells and textures. Basically getting them used to the world that we live in.

We need to guide them and help them to cope with things in the environment and keep their confidence up so you can have a well rounded dog when they are older.

Everyday life of sights we see, sounds we hear and scent we smell that we just take for granted. All of these have the potential of frightening your puppy. We do need to look at the world with new eyes when introducing our puppies to it.

Mini Outings

In the normal world where we weren't restricted to one form of exercise a day, I would be recommending to take you puppy out for mini sessions to get them used to the environment. To places such as Kenilworth (to those of you that are local) which is a small town. This allows your puppy to take in all sorts of things from people, shops, buses, pushchairs, cars and just life in general going on around him, but it not too crazy an environment to make sure we aren't overwhelming him.

When Maisie was a puppy I would take her out on mini outings to Kenilworth, pop to the bank, potter up the high street and just sit on a bench together letting her take in the environment paring it with food and just letting her take in the world. This has helped us when we go away to the Peak District camping as we often pop into a town like Bakewell which she is happy to potter around the small towns and go into the shops and we can also get to pop to the pub for a Sunday lunch too.

How are we going to do this during lockdown?

Don't think of your walk as getting out there and going as far as you can to see as much as you can in 30 minutes. You may end up potentially overwhelming his senses. Go at your puppies pace.

If your puppy is unsure and just wants to take in the world just on your road, don't worry that you haven't made it to the park — the walk is about the experience not how far you have been. Pick two things you want your puppy to experience each day, whether that is going to a new place or going people watching to prevent yourself from doing too much.

Body language

I am very mindful about what exposure my dogs get and I want you to be too. Pick and choose what experiences you want them to have and don't try to fit too much into a day as this could potentially cause him unnecessary stress and worry. Be mindful of not over exposing him to too much at once when he is learning and taking the world in.

You want to watch and see if your puppy is getting worried or stressed. If you see him hanging back, lip licking, tail under or shaking this may be too much for him. Give him a bit of distance from what is worrying him and if he wants to investigate further, go with him. If not try again another day but never force him through it — this will not make it a positive experience and in fact may make it worse.

Some puppies can be a little bit more sensitive than others, this is sometimes because of their genetic make up or their early experiences with their breeder. Just take it in their time, remember they are all individuals.

When I first became a dog walker I had a fab little Staffordshire bull terrier puppy I would take out on mini adventures to help him get used to the world for his owner. One day doing one of our regular walks there was a bucket randomly left in the middle of the pavement, it may as well have been a dragon standing in our way, not letting us past. He backed away barking at the bucket crouched down making himself look small. That day we just gave the bucket a wide berth, he wasn't ready to go any closer.

The next day the dragon bucket was there again, but today he was feeling braver, so we tacked the bucket together and I rewarded him for all o f his brave moves towards the bucket. The bucket was no longer a problem. This can just happen with puppies, one day an inanimate object is fine, the next day is may worry them, it's called a fear stage and they can go in and out of this through their puppyhood.

Making use of treats and toys will help you puppy pair the new experience with being a good one. Make sure you go out prepared and also have an idea on what you are going to be working on before you leave — remember the two things per day you are focusing on.

If you puppy cant be on the floor yet, you can still take them out you just need to carry them so they can still take in the sights, sounds and smells of a walk. Yes, there is less traffic, but there is still some going past.

Scattering some food on the floor as that car goes past will pair it with good stuff happening.

Playing with a toy when they can hear a dog barking close by will help them not be potentially worried by the noise.

Stand outside the front of your home on your doorstep or on your driveway and let them watch the world go by.

But we can only do this once a day?

Don't worry there is still lots you can do at home as well to build confidence and get them used to what I call novelty. We just need to be creative!

Do you own an 'Alexa'? Did you realise that it can play you city noises? It is an hour long recording of traffic, cars, people, etc. Have this playing on a low volume whilst you puppy is eating they meal or whilst they have a chew?

You don't, don't worry you can get these sounds from the Puppy Sound Proof app for any noises you don't have and make use of the internet. YouTube has recordings of many sounds which is going to be a great help to you right now.

Create a noise box or just pile your recycling on the floor, this may sound a bit crazy but puppy training doesn't need to be expensive and we can make use of what we have at home, you can make use of your recycling before throwing out away.

Cardboard boxes big and small, foil trays, plastic tubs, fruit packaging, bubble wrap, placates bags — anything you would normally recycle or throw away but has different textures and make different noises is great for this.

Other items you can use for confidence building are items from your cutlery draw, pots & pans, pie tins, measuring cups, metal spoons, bells, balls — any thing you have that will be novelty to your puppy and create different noises and has a range of textures — you can put them into the Noise Box or with the Recycling Rumble which is a obstacle.

How to play

For both games it's nice and simple, just throw treats in, around and on the various items you have out. What I would always suggest to use is some of their daily portion of food — ditch the bowl and make use of what they are already having anyway. The aim is to get them to investigate, knock around, knock over, walk on which will help build confidence with the noises it will make and all get them used to all the different textures. Asking them to walk over weird stuff and play with weird stuff and get them used to having different materials under their paws. When playing these games always remembering never to force your puppy, you can encourage them but try and let then investigate at their own pace.

Next, lets make use of your clothes line and use items that will make various noises and will move about over their head, start with tying plastics bags to the line, which are going to be 'new' things in the environment and as an added distraction for your puppy. No clothes line, no worries — just make use of your garden fence instead.

On your next essential trip out, pick up a bag of balloons and get everyone in your family to draw faces onto them and tie these onto your washing line or along your fence — anything novel for your puppy is going to grow their confidence and build that positive outlook on life.

Puppy Training doesn't have to be expensive

Lets make use too of the kids toys that you have in your home, get any toy that makes a noise, has flashing lights and get them running whilst you play with you puppy with all the novelty going on — have a novelty party! Let's add to the novelty party too, umbrellas, suitcase, hamper, hats, rain coats, sunglasses, back packs, umbrellas, gloves, fluorescent clothing — go through your seasonal wardrobe. Get your dog putting their head through items Anything you have in your home that isn't always sat out, get your novelty out!

Family Fun

Get the whole family involved in building your puppies confidence and get them trying on all your fancy dress items and wear around the house like its just a normal day — play dress up in whatever you already have. Anything weird and wonderful items you have in you home, Halloween outfits, costumes, masks, wigs, — put it on around your pup to make it seem absolutely normal — this is great novelty and creates weird silhouettes for your puppy.

When in fancy dress you can also practise some basic training with your puppy and have fun with them playing a game of tuggie to build that positive association for them.

Just so not to startle your puppy, don't put on a wig and a mask and then jump out form round a corner, it's not big and its not clever — just sit on the floor in with him and play a game of tug or do some fun food games. Particularly with masks or anything that makes you look very different, let them see you change into the new outfit as it will help him understand that people look different but they are still people even if you are slightly bonkers!

Everyday Life

We need them to get used to everyday household items and the sounds that they make and how they look and move like a vacuum cleaner, broom, washing machine, food processor - Throwing some treats on the floor whilst you are doing the hoovering or any of the other appliances being use can pair that positive association for your puppy.

Let's add motion to the equation and get out into your garden and ride bikes, push round your wheel barrow, skateboard on the drive, play with a ball, use spades, rakes, lawnmowers and hang up laundry to blow in the wind.

Sound and especially loud noises we need to work on when they are young to help teach your puppy that loud noises are not scary. Unfortunately is it a common problem in older dogs. We can reduce this potentially happening by creating a positive reaction to common problem noises.

Thunder, fireworks, hair dryers, vacuums, construction noises, children at playgrounds are just a few of the common noises dogs can be worried by.

- Have you treats at the ready and how you are going to play the sounds, whether that will be from your phone, a cd or you may use Alexa.
- Play the audio clip you are working on, for puppies that are more sensitive it should be early audible.
- Give your puppy a treat, press play and then give him a treat each second. This doesn't need to be 'treats' you can just use

part of their daily portion of food. Just before your puppy finishes the food stop the audio.

- Make this a non event and start to vary the time in which you give the treats, play with the treat before giving it to them, offer nothing and then get one. What we want it is the audio to be the prediction that food is on its way.

Just because we have distance in place, doesn't mean you cant go to the super market with your partner and sit in the car with your puppy and watch the world go by with your puppy whilst they get the fun job of shopping.

Sit in your front garden or just observe people form your front door or window.

Even the most confident of puppies go through the fear stage in their development and this happens more than once or twice, with Maisie I saw her go in and out of the fear stages multiple time in the first two years of her life.

Be prepared

I always suggest to have treats ready in your pocket ready, so you can pair any loud noises with food when they happen.

Creating a diary is super helpful, what you exposure you have done with your puppy and how they react to it — so you can see where their confidence is and what you may need to work on with them too.

One of my clients kept a detailed dairy of what they did with their puppy, what worried them what they loved to help them with getting them used to the world. They also found it super useful for keeping a note to speed up toilet training too.

Have fun and remember quality not quantity. We want our puppies used to novelty and for it to not be a 'big thing' b y creating those positive experiences.

Take pictures and cherish the moments, they are not a puppy for long and while this time round it may not be a normal puppy upbringing it will still be awesome and fun and you will miss the tiny puppy when they are all grown up — so enjoy them whilst you can.

Crate Training - How to stop your dog from peeing, chewing and rampaging your home

RAISING A PUPPY during lockdown, we must make sure that he spends a bit of the day away from you each day ie pop him in his crate for a nap or with something to do, like a kong or chew. If he gets used to you being around all the time, which may be for weeks that may potentially turn into months until things go back to normal when you eventually go back to work, he may potentially struggle with being on his own.

Even if you can be him all the time, you should still build this into your daily routine and practise some alone time. After weeks of not leaving your side, going back to normal will undoubtedly have a big impact on your puppy.

Puppies are not born comfortable with being left on their own, we need to teach them that it's no big deal and it just happens sometimes. We should not just expect them to 'deal with it' and they will just have to get used to it, we need to help them understand that it's ok.

This is why it is important to crate train your puppy, especially in lockdown, but additionally they are a great tool to use to help you house train your puppy and great prevention to stop them from chewing all of your furniture. Management is going to be your best friend when brining up a puppy.

Crate Size

The size of the crate is very important, as needs to be big enough for your puppy to lay down and stretch, but not so big that there is enough space to sleep at one end and toilet in the other. And yes, you will need to buy a new crate as your puppy grows. The other option is to have a larger crate and put a divider in it to reduce the space they have.

Crate training needs to start on the first day when you bring your puppy home, but not as soon as you walk in your home as picking them up! Don't just pop them straight in there and expect him to be ok with it, because they won't be and you'll just end up with a crying pup.

Too Much Advice

You've told friends that you have decided to crate train your new puppy and they all had their own advice and tips to give to you, it seems to differ from one person to the next and everyone seems to be an expert these days. Just remember, it doesn't make them an expert just because they've raised one puppy!

'We didn't have them in our day and our dog turned out ok!'

'Our puppy hated it and we gave up after two nights of crying'

Every dog if different but I do have a plan to set you and your puppy up for success. Let's get you started on the right paw using a crate, here are my tops tips of how to make it the best place for your puppy to be

1. Don't put your pup straight in the crate when you get them home! Have the crate ready for them and let them investigate it in their own time.
2. Expectations - lower them. Don't expect your pup to be able to sleep all night straight away. At 8 weeks old they do not yet have full control of their bladder. Please let them out for a final toilet and then pop them to bed as late as possible, get up

approx 4 hours later, pick them up out of their crate, put them out in the garden and wait for them to toilet, praise with a treat then put straight back in the crate. This must be a non-event, you need to be as boring as possible, put them on a lead if you need to which will prevent any running around and waking themselves up and having fun. You can start to extend the 4 hours gradually as you think they are getting more control of their bladder as they grow until eventually, they can go the whole night.

3. Every time your pup falls asleep pop them into their crate, so that they wake up every time in there. I know it's lovely to have puppy cuddles when they fall asleep on you, but think in the long run? Do you want to have to be there every time for your puppy to settle and fall asleep?

4. Feed all of their meals in there, give them treats/chews in the crate. This makes the crate an amazing place where they get yummy treats and good stuff happens!

5. Never use your crate for a time out , it does not teach your dog anything and it will make them hate their crate.

6. Play crate games. These will help your dog to love their crate! There is a game below to get you started.

7. On your puppy's first night in your home, either have the crate in your room or sleep on the sofa with the crate close by. If they cry, just pop your hand next to the crate to let them know you are there with some gentle words to help soothe and settle them. They will be frightened and just need some reassurance and don't worry you can not reinforce fear. After a few nights once they are settled and happy in their crate, you can start moving the crate away from you and gradually move them to their final sleeping place (ie the kitchen or laundry room)

8. When you can't watch your pup, pop them in their crate with something to do, like a stuffed kong. This is a great management tool to prevent the chewing and causing destruction in your home when you can't have your beady eye on them.

9. Play more crate games, I think this is key to make them love their crate!

10. Cover their crate as it makes it into a den for them to feel safe in.

11. If they go into their crate on their own accord, don't bother

them and leave them to settle. Make it a rule for the kids to leave the puppy alone if they go into their crate.

12. House training will be easier, dogs do not like to mess in their space, their crate soon becomes a space they don't want to toilet in. When you are toilet training and can't keep an eye on them, pop them in the crate but remember to make sure you have met their needs before popping them in there and to take them straight in the garden when you take them out of their crate to give them a chance to toilet.

13. Always provide your dog fresh drinking water on their crate, even if they seem to knock it over every night and is makes a mess. If this is irritating you, there are bowls available that attach to the side of the crate to prevent this. Dogs must always have access to fresh water, please do not take it away in the hope they won't need to toilet in the night.

When your puppy goes to the groomers, needs to stay at the vet's or has a dog walker it will be easier for them to deal with the new situation as you have spent time to work on this and they love their crate.

Please remember, when you bring home your puppy they are in a new environment where his puppy family haven't come with him. There are scary strangers that he doesn't know and that speak in another language.

Put yourself in their paws and think about how they may be feeling. Lower your expectations, learn how to talk to each other and enjoy your new bundle of fluff!

Introduce a crate correctly and they will love it for life and it has many benefits!

I was 24 and working part-time in a pub when I adopted Tye from The Dog's Trust and he was my first own dog. We had a family dog called Crystal when I was young, but Tye was my own and I was going to be the best dog owner for him.

I prepared and read up before I got him home, borrowed a crate and had all the essentials ready for his arrival. This was a long time before I became a dog trainer and I didn't fully understand how much of my time he would take up or how hard it could be at times.

When I brought him home I straight away realised the crate was far too small for him, so we wouldn't be able to use it. He was 4 months old when I re-homed him and already a good size and ended up to be a pretty large dog, weighing in a 7 and a half stone when he was fully grown.

Instead of the crate he had his own boudoir, ok it was just our laundry room where his bed was kept and where he slept at night.

There was a big learning curve for me for sure, I will be the first to admit I didn't realise how much of my time this awesome new puppy would take up and how I needed to keep an eye on him all the time.

Things he stole and chewed are quite an extensive list but included glasses, cupboards, chair legs, tables, a remote control, wires, a watch, bras, socks and pants are to name a few. He was also allowed too much free-roaming as a puppy, I didn't always keep him with me in the same room and I may have once or twice had a nana nap and woke up to him chewing something new.

Managing his access and using a crate would have helped me so much and there would have been less of 'what has that dog got now'. It was never his fault he was just finding his own job to keep himself entertained, he became self-employed. Dogs do like to chew too, its reinforcing to them, it makes them feel good which is why they do it, we just need to be managing them and providing them appropriate outlets.

It was my fault for not keeping a close enough eye on him or putting him in a safe confined area where he couldn't chew my house and its contents and I promised myself it wouldn't happen again,

When Maisie came into my life, she was introduced to the crate the day I brought her home and I made sure for her it a fab place to be so she was happy and comfortable in there. This meant I was able to manage her behaviour pretty well too. The only item she ever chewed was a pair of flip flops that I kept in the downstairs back room, when someone else left the door open and she got in there.

How do I help them love their crate?

As well as making it the best place to be by using chews and feeding them in there, you can play crate games which will supercharge their love for their crate.

Crate Game - you're in, you're out

- Encourage your puppy into their crate using a treat
- Reward your puppy with a few treats by placing them in the crate on the floor
- As your puppy is eating the treats, shut the door closed
- When he is eating the last one, open up the crate and reward him at the back corner of the crate, so this encourages him to the back of the crate, but also into a sit.
- Repeat the above a few times. What you are doing is building the crate to be a very valuable place.
- The next time, open the crate door and hold the treat near your puppies nose and throw the treat away from the crate, so your puppy comes out of the crate and chases the treat
- Your puppy will then come back to you to see where the next one is coming from, wist hem out they may choose on their own to go back into the crate. If they don't, not to worry, just use a treat get your puppy to follow it back into the crate and again place a few treats on the crate floor for a puppy to find and repeat the above a few more times
- Repeat the above of opening and shutting the door and reward him at the back corner of the crate, so this encourages him to the back of the crate, but also into the sit that we are after.
- This time I want you moving the locks across as well and you standing up a little away from the crate rather than just being crochet next to the crate
- Now and again, open the crate door and show your puppy the 1 treat and throw out away from the crate to encourage your puppy out
- What you are doing is building lots of value for being in the crate and not too much value for being out of the crate, lots of treats in the crate and only 1 treat out of the crate

- What will start to happen is you won't need to use a treat to get your puppy to go into the crate they will do it on their own.

To build on this you want to be able to go out of the room, so when your puppy is busy with a chew or a toy in their crate or pen, just go out of sight around the corner. Then come straight back so it's not too overwhelming for your puppy. If your puppy is comfortable with this, slowly increase the time you're out of the room. You can also play you're in, you're out too building up the distance you go away from the crate and building in time too.

The key is to start this now, our dogs have gotten used to us being around more so we need to start preparing them that we won't be around all day and getting them loving their crate. Make a plan and use my guidelines below to make a plan for the next week of getting your puppy used to you not being on tap all day. You want your lockdown puppy to get used to spending time on their own in their crate, but first you must make sure you have met your puppies needs. Has he been fed, exercised and been to the toilet?

Yes? That's great but do not just pop them straight in there after a walk, you need your pup to be calm when doing this training. Is your puppy now calm? Then now you can begin. To start we are going to provide them something to do. Like a chew or a kong to start, as you won't be going far and will be able to hear them. Start off where you puppy is happy to be left, this may be just 1 minute, just start where your puppy is comfortable. You are going to build this up daily up to 2 hours, but do not try on day one try and do 2 hours as this would be too much too quick.

Don't make a fuss when you pop them in there and leave some white noise on for him, such as a radio. Time yourself, walk away but stay in the room and go back after 1 minute and let your just let him out, quick fuss and go back to watching the tv so he will follow you.

We want this to be a non-event and your aim is to build up slowly, so that he never gets a chance or whine and that he is happy to be left in there. You may be able to start for longer than 1 minute, go by what your puppy is comfortable with. Once you have built this up successfully to 2 hours with you straying in the house, you are ready for the next step.

Our next step is for you to leave the house and for your puppy to be ok with you going out the front door. To do this through, you need to reduce your criteria again (sorry dog training word!) You just need to make it easier for him to get success, so back down to just 1 minute (or less if needed). Then build up slowly again. I know what you are thinking, what am I supposed to do for two hours outside the from of my home? Go and sit in your car and listen to a podcast, read a book or listen to the radio with a cup of coffee.

Again through, when you go back in make sure it's a calm release from the crate, a quick hello and make another cup of coffee.

If your puppy is struggling, you can start this when going to the toilet, leave a small handful of treats outside the door don't shut the door fully to start just push it to. When they have finished eating you will be back. This is starting the process of building up distance from you with less pressure. Build this up to going for a shower with the door shut whilst they eat a kong outside the door and then move onto the crate.

Additional strategies for success

Other ways you can increase the time of them being on their own, when you make dinner leave them in another room in a pen or crate, water the plants in your garden and you watch them on a camera whilst you read a book or you could sit in the garden if it is a nice day. Slowly increase the time you are gone as long as your puppy doesn't show signs of distress.

Build it up slowly, don't try and rush it in a few days. Rome wasn't built in a day.

Remember you need to go at your puppies pace for all of my 3 easy steps to success, quality not quantity.

About The Author

THIS IS THE part of the book that not many will read, so I could potentially write anything in here. A s long as there are words here to fill the space, it could be flicked past to see what freebies I am leaving you with on the next page.

I could use this page to tell you all about my business Carrie's Canines & Friends that I have been running since 2016, along with help from my assistants. How I love to help dog owners improve their walks by adding in games and mental stimulation to create calmer dogs whilst owners at work, so they don't need to worry. The lovely cats I get to care for when their owners are away on their holidays. Or the training I do with clients in classes our 1:1 and see the lightbulbs go off in the owners head (and the dogs heads) to as they 'get it' and grow a love for training their dogs and realise how awesome dogs are and that I am Coventry's No1 Puppy Training Specialist.

Maybe I should be telling you that I went to University in Lincoln to study Fashion Studies where I got my degree after college, that I ended up staying there until I was 24 and then I relocated back to Coventry in search of a career making use of my degree. Two years later I ended up with a potential career in the fashion industry working at Sainsburys head office, where I stayed for 5 years. Before my epiphany to change careers, as if I didn't do it now I will never do it when I was in my early 30's to be a dog walker and that 1 year later, I went back to studying to retrain myself to become a dog trainer and behaviourist.

How about that I live in Coventry with my two dogs, Maisie a collie x spaniel who is 5 and Eric a cavapoo who is 3 and once you get me talking about my own dogs I may not stop and then the pictures may come out too.

Or I could give you my CV - but really how boring would that be?

A lovely lady called Vicky Fraser who inspired me to write this book (when I first met her I said I will never write a book and look where I am now) and how she ended her book with interesting things about her, is what I am going to share with you about me today. Some of the things I love and, well hate is a strong word, but a dislike them very much!

Things I love - the smell of freshly cut grass, camping with my dogs and friends, days out walking in Peak District or in the countryside, spending time with friends whether that is on a camping break, at a festival or at the pub.

Laughter with friends family and well anyone I meet, being in the great outdoors, chocolate (does not need any explanation I only know of one person that dislikes it), BBQ's.

Training my dogs, dog cuddles, the smell of tiny puppy paws, flip flops, being barefoot, curled up inside on a cold wet day, early frosty sunny morning walks, Sunday lunch, watching dogs brains work, beer garden weather, the beach, being out dog walking with clients dogs, watching the seasons changes, bluebells in the woods, watching leaves bud up in spring, wearing hoodies, painting my nails, dressing up for a night out, being in my pjs, being at my home, travelling abroad, eating foods from different countries, buying books...too many books, my kindle, listening to books, music, dancing, more laughter, bands, printed leggings, glitter and sequins, fancy dress and my now love writing.

Things I don't partially like - having wet socks, not being able to sleep, driving in the dark, wet dog smell, really boggy muddy woodland walks, falling over in said mud, having a weak ankle, being closer to 40 than 30, being away from my dogs, cheesy 80's music and 90's RnB, the smell of tripe, having muddy floors and not seeing my friends enough.

Now you know more about me and my world and the tiny space I take up in it, what things do you love?

Your Free Gifts

THESE 3 STEPS I have shared with you alone will help you not only survive lockdown with your puppy, but thrive. They will ensure your puppy gets started on the right paw or your lives together, even in these uncertain times.

The advice I have shared is just part of a more comprehensive unique Puppy Problem Prevention Programme where my 10 step system guides you for A to B, so from settling in your new puppy on his first night at home to meeting your family, toilet training to biting and walking by your side to recall to help you bring up the perfect pup.

Please don't try and wait until the situation has changed and social distancing has been reduced, as that could potentially be in 3 months time in which your puppy problem will be affecting your daily lives together.

Ignoring a problem like jumping up or mouthing won't make it go away. They won't just grown out of it.

The more chance they get to practise it, the more likely they are going to keep doing it for the rest of their life. It becomes an ingrained behaviour.

Let's get you started with your Special free gifts.

My first free gift for you, well more for your puppy is a yummy, easy to make 'puppy cake' recipe that you can use to keep your puppy's focus locked onto you. I love to encourage you to make use of your puppies daily allowance of food to do their training, by ditching the food bowl. But just sometimes it just doesn't cut the mustard. You may need something more for your puppy to use when out on walks, as the world can sometimes be a scary place and we need to be banking up those good experiences. I am sharing with you Maisie Moo's Liver Cake Recipe for you to download and make.

My second gift for you which is my Personalised Puppy Homeschooling Diary for you to print out and pop on your fridge. It is a chart to keep on top of your puppy training. It will help you and your family housetrain your puppy sooner, help you all know when the puppy has been fed, how much sleep they are having and what training has been done.

My third gift is my Essential Items New Puppy Shopping List for your new puppy. Many dog owners buy a lot of things they don't need, but I will keep it simple for you with my essentials that you need for when they come home. You have their whole lives to spoil them, try not to go overboard right from the start.

My fourth gift to you is my Fast Track Perfect Puppy Manners Video Series, so you can start teaching your puppy some polite manners. Three ways to stop your puppy jumping up and how to teach your puppy to sit.

Access all you free gifts from me here   https://www.carriescanines.co.uk/puppyresources/

I hope you have enjoyed my book and have found my special free gifts useful.

If you want to avoid all the mistake most inexperiences puppy owners make, then you should join Carries Online Puppy Home School Program.

You still get ALL the help and guidance you need exactly as you would in a normal classroom, it will just be done remotely online. In many ways this is better for you than attending a regular puppy class, as you'll get my personal help to work through your struggles, and your puppy won't be distracted by other puppies in the room. You just do it at home instead of in a classroom.

I will ask you to film your sessions to make sure you are on the right track to getting that puppy you were dreaming of. Guidance and support will always be there for you, where you'll get my personal help to get you through this difficult time.

Carries Puppy Home School runs on a 6-week course, which also enrols you into my private 'exclusive' online club where you have access to my private Facebook community where ask me questions whenever you need me. This gives you access to a weekly live to answer any questions and help with problems you may face with your new puppy.

Let's ensure you bring up the perfect pup. Spaces are limited on these courses, which will ensure you and your puppy get the individual attention you need.

As an extra thank you to you for investing time in this book, you can have the above programme's at 50% off, just input the code PERFECTPUPPY when booking. https://www.carriescanines.co.uk/puppyhomeschool/

Printed in Poland
by Amazon Fulfillment
Poland Sp. z o.o., Wrocław

58528669R00027